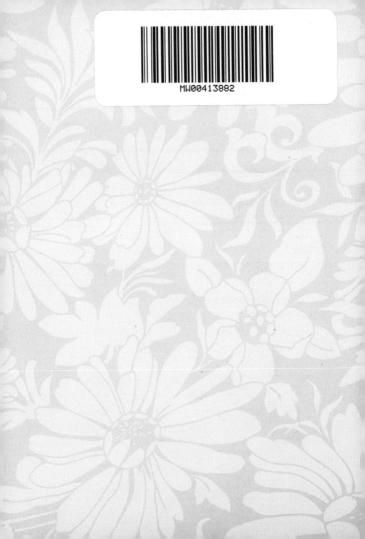

MW00413882

Rob & Susan Cottrell

HopeMinute

One minute that will change your day

60 Devotions

summerside

Summerside Press
Minneapolis 55438
www.summersidepress.com

HopeMinute: One minute that will change your day
© 2010 by Rob and Susan Cottrell
Additional entries by Josh Taylor, Jeff Osborne, and Amy Oldham.

ISBN 978-1-935416-62-3

Scripture references are from the following sources: The Holy Bible, English Standard Version® (ESV), copyright © 2001 by Crossway Bibles, a publishing ministry of Good News Publishers. Used by permission. All rights reserved. The New King James Version (NKJV). Copyright © 1982 by Thomas Nelson, Inc. Used by permission. THE HOLY BIBLE, NEW INTERNATIONAL VERSION®. NIV®. Copyright © 1973, 1978, 1984 by International Bible Society. Used by permission of Zondervan Publishing House. The New Century Version (NCV), copyright © 2005 by Thomas Nelson, Inc. Used by permission. All rights reserved. The Holy Bible, New Living Translation (NLT), copyright © 1996, 2004. Used by permission of Tyndale House Publishers, Inc., Wheaton, Illinois 60189. All rights reserved. *The Message.* Copyright © 1993, 1994, 1995, 1996, 2000, 2001, 2002 by Eugene Peterson. Used by permission of NavPress Publishing Group.

Cover and interior design by Thinkpen Design, Inc.
Cover photo 2009 Shutterstock.

Summerside Press™ is an inspirational publisher offering fresh, irresistible books to uplift the heart and engage the mind.

Printed in China.

To my children Christopher, Andrea, Natalie, David, and Hannah...thank you. You have shared your Daddy with so many children—at a significant sacrifice. God will bless your hearts. I can't imagine better children. You are everything I could ever want. I love you more than you know, more than I have shown.

Wherever there is life, there is hope...always.
Hope is a powerful medicine.

Robert Cottrell

"Hope is a powerful medicine. Those are not my words but I completely believe in them. The words of hope in *HopeMinute* carry a message that empowers, uplifts, and encourages anyone who reads it. At a time when many want to toss in the towel, a message of love and compassion telling us that there is light at the end of the tunnel is what we need to carry the ball just a little bit further."

Tom Lehman
1996 PGA Tour Player of the Year
and author of *A Passion for the Game*

"An intriguing book captivating hope, encouragement, and the pursuit of faith."

Hon. Dean Martin
Arizona State Treasurer

*"Sometimes God
will calm the storms
and sometimes
He will give us strength
to get through it."*

CONTENTS

Hope Is My Heart

I have been blessed with the chance to sit quietly with people whose lives have been turned upside down by cancer. I have met with children one-on-one, with family members and close friends, and with whole families together. Sometimes we cry, sometimes we laugh, but we are always hopeful. These dear people share every feeling, every hope, every dream. I listen to them and they listen to me, and together we develop a relationship that transcends my role as the leader of a charitable organization. We become friends. We become family.

HopeMinute is an outgrowth of caring for that family relationship. It is intended to be a companion. I hope that as you read through it, you will sense that in us you have friends—people who understand how hard it is to get through the hard days, hours, minutes. Our desire is that *HopeMinute* will be the one minute that will change your day. The one minute that will color the rest of your day with hope.

Rob Cottrell

The Meaning of Hope

HopeWord

> *But as for me, I will always have hope;*
> *I will praise you more and more.*
> *My mouth will tell of your righteousness,*
> *of your salvation all day long,*
> *though I know not its measure.*
>
> PSALM 71:14–15 NIV

HopeMinute

Hope. A simple word. A powerful truth. A miraculous healing medicine. That is what hope means to me. But does that fit with the dictionary definition of the word?

According to the Cambridge dictionary: 1. Hope (noun)—Something good that you want to happen in the future, or a confident feeling about what will happen in the future. I like that one. Something good that you want to happen and a confident feeling that

11

it really will happen! 2. Hope (verb)—To want something to happen or to be true, and usually to have a good reason to think that it might. I like this one too! A desire for something to happen, but not an empty dream. We have a good reason to think that it might come true.

Another way to look at Hope is by exploring its synonyms: 1. Anticipation or expectancy—A pleasurable expectation. 2. Hopefulness, encouragement, optimism—The feeling and belief that all is going to turn out well. 3. Promise, expectation—A belief about or a mental picture of the future. What powerful words. What an amazing way to live.

These definitions hint at the importance of hope. But it is so much more. The reality defines description. It is personal, spiritual, life-saving.

Living each day with hope can change your entire outlook. I can't imagine life without hope. What impact might that have on your life? On the life of those around you? To live life with the firm, strong, grounded belief that the future is long and healthy.

Live life with hope. Live a hopeful life. It is powerful medicine.

RC

HopePrayer

Lord, You are the author of hope, the object and only reason for hope. Lord, remind me to hope in You—not in me, nor my circumstances—but in You, the author and finisher of my faith.

Ready for Love

The only thing that counts is
faith expressing itself through love.

GALATIANS 5:6 NIV

Recently, I watched *Little Women*, the old movie with Katharine Hepburn. It's charming. What I loved was a line from the main character, Jo. She had turned down a proposal from Laurie, her neighbor, breaking his heart. Some time later she says, "I think I would accept his proposal now. Love means more to me now than it did then."

Love means a lot—more than we can accurately communicate. But when we are young, we often take it for granted, expecting it always to be there. The older we get—at least the older I get—the more we realize that love is extremely precious. We assume the ones we love will be here forever, but that is not guaranteed. We assume we will always be loved, but that is not guaranteed either. We can, however, always count on the love of God.

Today—right this minute—take the time to express your love to those who are important to you. Tell your loved ones how blessed you are to have them in your life. Thank God for them. Don't wait. Then be ready for the full value of love.   SC

HopePrayer

Lord, thank You for Your love—it is all I need. Yet, You've put others around me who love me, and I thank You for them. Lord, help me appreciate those who love me. Help me show them Your love, powerfully and tangibly. I love You, Lord.

It Is All In the Timing

God will always give what is right to his people who cry to him night and day, and he will not be slow to answer them. I tell you, God will help his people quickly. But when the Son of Man comes again, will he find those on earth who believe in him?

LUKE 18:7-8 NCV

HopeMinute

Why does God sometimes wait until the sickness has lingered? Why does God sometimes wait until the money is gone? Why does God sometimes not heal people on this side of the heaven? I don't know. I only know that His timing is always right. I can only say that He will do what is best. Always.

Although you hear nothing, He is speaking. Although you see nothing, He is working. With God there are no accidents. Every situation we face is intended to help

16

us know more about Him and know more of His love for us. His time for answering our prayers is always the perfect time for what we need.

No matter what is happening in your life right now, God has a plan. He knows what you will be facing today and He will take care of you. You may question when. It is all in the timing. His timing is impeccable.

Hang on. Trust. Believe. God is for you.   RC

HopePrayer

God, are You there? I'm at the end of my rope here. Oh yes, that's when I get to see You work, when I come to depend on You more. Show me Your sufficiency, Lord.

Listening to the Heart

> *Pay close attention to what you hear.*
> *The closer you listen, the more understanding you*
> *will be given—and you will receive even more.*

MARK 4:24 NLT

HopeMinute

Am I a good listener? Sometimes. Am I a good listener to my kids? Probably not. I am more likely considered a good lecturer. Good listening means paying attention, not merely waiting for your chance to air your grievances.

Listening is more than the absence of talking. It doesn't involve multi-tasking or daydreaming or looking elsewhere. I am so guilty of not really listening to my kids. I continue to read the paper, type e-mail, wash the dishes, or plan the grocery list while my children are telling me something. I am sure I do the same thing to a lot of other people.

Listening is the active process of hearing what people are saying. It means looking in their eyes, paying attention to body language, and then processing all that to determine what's really being said. A good listener asks follow-up questions to determine what's in the heart. When we really listen, the person talking will feel, at least for that moment, like the most important person in the world.

We are all often scared and nervous about what the future holds. By listening and really hearing we give comfort. Whether we are listening to a friend, a sermon, or a repetitive child, the important part is hearing their heart.

RC

HopePrayer

Lord, I admit I sometime have trouble listening. I pray that You help me listen, even when I'm busy, even if I don't like what someone is saying. You have asked me to listen, and I pray that You will remind me, strengthen me, and focus me to listen.

Seize the Day!

HopeWord

> *There is surely a future hope for you,*
> *and your hope will not be cut off.*
>
> PROVERBS 23:18 NIV

HopeMinute

We may cherish our yesterdays, or even regret them, but we can never live them again. The past is behind us; the future lies ahead. The future is real and promising; the past is neither of those things. Only by looking to the future with hope can we deal with the past.

Sometimes, however, as we look to the future, our hope gets dimmed and we long for the better days gone by. To find only positives in the past and negatives in the future can rob us of one of our greatest gifts: time. And time is one thing the past can't give us. We have time now. Today. Taking advantage of it is how we keep hope alive.

Yesterday's gifts are memories. They are precious. But we can only grow mentally and spiritually by living in this day, living in this moment with our eyes focused on greater things and a hopeful future. No matter what the past or future hold for us, we have today, right now, to live.

Our hope is in what is to come next. God has given us that promise. His promises are solid. So we can live this day with exuberance. We can seize *this* day. Our future hope is secure in Him.

RC

HopePrayer

Show me what You have for me *this* day, Lord. Fill me with Your peace *this* day. Please heal my regrets for the past, calm my fears of the future, and live through me *this* day.

At Home with God

> *Then Christ will make his home in your hearts*
> *as you trust in him. Your roots will grow down*
> *into God's love and keep you strong.*
>
> Ephesians 3:17–19 NLT

HopeMinute

Regardless of our beliefs, when tragedy strikes close to home, we look for answers and we turn to God. But, there may be something that you have not yet come to realize. God wants to be your dwelling place. He has no interest in being a weekend getaway or a Sunday bungalow or a summer cottage. Don't consider using God as a vacation cabin or eventual retirement home. He wants you under His roof now and always. He wants to be your mailing address, your point of reference. He wants to be your home.

For many, this is a new thought. We think of God as a deity to discuss, not a place to dwell. We think of God as a mysterious miracle worker, not a house to live in. We think of God as a creator to call on, not a home to reside in.

Our Father wants to be much more. He wants to be the One in whom "we live and move and have our being." Why? Because He loves us, works all things out for our good, and has a perfect plan for us. He wants to be with us.

If this is indeed a new thought for you, simply open your heart and ask God to reveal Himself to you. You just need to make yourself at home. He will take care of the rest.

RC

HopePrayer

Ah! I am relaxing in Your home for me, Lord. You have provided food and water and rest. Please keep me here with You, not venturing off somewhere else. It sure is beautiful here!

Lessons Learned

> *I applied my heart to what I observed*
> *and learned a lesson from what I saw.*
>
> PROVERBS 24:32 NIV

HopeMinute

Ben Franklin once admonished us to "Learn from everyone." I like Mr. Franklin's idea. To take the time to learn from someone is to acknowledge that they have value. It's a way of appreciating who they are, even if you are traveling on a very different road. It isn't as easy to learn when we think the teacher has little to offer. But there is a reason for everyone who has crossed our path, a lesson to learn from each person.

My older sister has taught me countless things over the years: generosity, patience, kindness, and the list goes on. There have been times when I have hated to admit that she could teach me anything—but she has, and does. As she faces the second half of life, she is teaching me even more than before. We can still learn from each other.

I am also learning from a friend who is twenty years younger than I am. From her I have learned to love and trust the Lord with my whole heart. She hungers to know God more fully, even when life is tough and painful. Even though she is young, she continually teaches and challenges me.

I need to take the time to consider what I can learn from each person who crosses my path. I challenge you to do the same. I think that if we are not learning, we are pretty much done growing—mentally and spiritually. Everyone has something to teach if we will only pay attention.

As long as we keep learning, there is hope for tomorrow. Hope for new cures. Hope for changes in fortune. Hope for tomorrow. I am holding on to that hope. sc

HopePrayer

Lord, thank You that I am never finished learning. I pray that my heart will be supple and open to whatever teacher You put in my path.

A Crisp View of God

> *Lord, even when I have trouble all around me,*
> *you will keep me alive.*
>
> PSALM 138:7 NCV

HopeMinute

There is a window in your heart through which you can see God. Once upon a time that window was clear. Your view of God was crisp. You could see God as vividly as you could see a valley or hillside.

Then the window cracked. A pebble of pain broke the clear window. And suddenly God was not so easy to see. The view that had been so crisp changed. Were you puzzled? Did you wonder how God could allow something like that to happen to your family?

When you can't see Him clearly, when you are confused and disappointed, when you are scared, just trust Him. Although your window has changed, God has not. God is closer than you've ever dreamed.

Also remember that you can always go to Him just as you are. There is no need to wait until you clean up your act or when you are on your best behavior. Trust Him right where you are, right when you need Him. He will give you a peace that passes all understanding—especially in difficult times. He is the author of hope.

RC

HopePrayer

Lord, would You please restore that clear glass? Fix the broken window and wipe it clean. Help me see You clearly again. I want to see You. I miss You.

Contentment

HopeWord

> *I have learned the secret of being content in any*
> *and every situation, whether well fed or hungry,*
> *whether living in plenty or in want. I can do every-*
> *thing through him who gives me strength.*
>
> PHILIPPIANS 4:12–13 NIV

HopeMinute

There are times when the one thing you want is the one thing you never get.

You pray and wait. No answer. You pray and wait. Then you start questioning things. What if God says no? What if the request is delayed? If God does say no, how will you respond? If God says, "I've given you My grace, and that is enough in this situation," how do you deal with that? Will you be content?

Content. That's an interesting word. It is basically a state of heart in which you would be at peace if God gave you nothing more than He already has. It is being able to accept the situation as it is and knowing that God will give you the strength to get through it.

Contentment often is not easy, but in it we will indeed find rest. God gives us the strength we need in every situation—even when He says no. Call on Him to give you the peace that you need.   RC

HopePrayer

God, I have no control over this situation. My contentment must come from You. You know the desires of my heart, but I surrender to You, asking for Your peace, even if nothing changes. Teach me to be content in any and every situation. Thank You, Lord.

A Compassionate Father

> *He comforts us every time we have trouble,*
> *so when others have trouble,*
> *we can comfort them*
> *with the same comfort God gives us.*

2 CORINTHIANS 1:4 NCV

HopeMinute

When my child's feelings are hurt, I tell her she's special. When my child is injured, I do whatever it takes to make her feel better. When my child is afraid, I won't go to sleep until she is secure.

I'm not a hero. I'm a Dad. When a child hurts, a parent does what comes naturally. He or she helps. Usually we don't even think about it.

Sometimes I wonder why I don't let my Father God do for me what I am more than willing to do for my own children.

Being a father is teaching me that when I am criticized, injured, or afraid, there is indeed someone greater, my Father God, who is ready to comfort me. Someone who will hold me until I'm better, who will help me until I can live with the hurt, and who won't go to sleep when I'm afraid of waking up and seeing the dark.

There is a Father who won't let go of me. Ever.   RC

HopePrayer

Oh Lord, life can be hard and scary and overwhelming. God, I thank You that You won't *ever* leave me. And please remind me, when I forget, that You are God and that You won't let me go.

There Is a Plan

> *"For I know the plans I have for you," declares the*
> *Lord, "plans to prosper you and not to harm you,*
> *plans to give you hope and a future."*
>
> JEREMIAH 29:11 NIV

HopeMinute

Let's face it. Some seasons of life are just hard. Some days seem to have stress lurking around every corner. When things get really tough, we often like to hide from the real life drama around us. We know it's not a healthy way to live, but we do it anyway. We try to zone out, deny, escape, or drown out the issues.

It is important to remember that the temporary fixes or worldly comforts we turn to will indeed go away, be spent, or dry up quickly. And we will again be faced with the pain. Instead, we can choose to live life on God's terms, bringing enthusiasm and passion into our lives. Our decision to trust and our decision to love life, despite the highs and lows, allows us to delight in the triumphs and to accept the disappointments as unavoidable—but momentary—setbacks.

When we focus on the fact that there is a plan for our lives—a plan for each day—we are better equipped to handle the drama. Sometimes it doesn't make sense and sometimes we don't understand how the plan works. Our job is to trust, to live life with gusto. Choosing to maintain our enthusiasm and passion for life, even if we don't understand the whole plan, will bring a joy and a peace that passes understanding.   RC

HopePrayer

Dear Lord, I do get stressed. Help me through the stress, not by changing the circumstances (which may or may not happen), but by healing me (which is always available). I want to see Your plan for this if You are willing. But with or without it, I pray that You still give me enthusiasm and passion for life. Thank You, Lord.

The Power of Words

> *How sweet are your words to my taste,*
> *sweeter than honey to my mouth!*
>
> PSALM 119:103 NIV

HopeMinute

I remember encouraging words. When I was ten, my sister told me how well I removed the tablecloth from the table without spilling any crumbs. When I was fourteen, my niece told me admiringly that she thought I was pretty. When I was eighteen, my father admired the way I figured out a logic riddle.

How easy it is to give words of affirmation. You simply voice out loud those positive observations you make about others. We have no way of knowing which ones will stick, but I believe encouraging words are never wasted. Who knows, a person may remember a simple compliment for decades. I know I did!

I remember discouraging words, too, like the names my six-grade classmates called me. Oh, God has healed those hurts, but there is a lot of staying power for words carelessly tossed out.

We almost can't help forming our self-opinions from the building blocks of what others tell us. Calling a child clumsy or fat or stupid may seem innocent enough to the speaker, but those words bore in deep and hang on for years. A proverb claims that careless words go like a morsel down to the inmost being. In that case, shouldn't we be careful what we say to those who are listening intently?

When I was twelve, I looked up to my kind neighbor, a principal at a nearby school. She admired a story I'd written, commenting on my vivid description of the main character and details of the story's events. Decades later that memory brings a smile to my face. Not only did she encourage me greatly, she also gave me a vision of myself as a good writer. She saw me as more than I saw myself. Her words actually cast a vision for me and for my future.

I try not to miss many opportunities to speak kind words, especially to children. I try to use words that raise self-confidence. It only takes a bit of focusing on the person. It is not hard to do. Besides, you never know when you will cast a vision into someone's life. Words are powerful.

SC

HopePrayer

Lord, please speak through me kind words You want me to say. Remind me to see the beauty in others and to then verbalize that. Thank You for the many wonderful and encouraging words You have said to me.

Watch, Wait, and Hope

HopeWord

We wait in hope for the Lord;
he is our help and our shield.
In him our hearts rejoice,
for we trust in his holy name.
May your unfailing love rest upon us, O Lord,
even as we put our hope in you.

PSALM 33:20–22 NIV

HopeMinute

How do we best support someone in their hour of need? We watch, wait, and hope. However, there are some requirements: a close relationship, attentive presence, time, patience, openness, and listening. If we are willing to invest the time, we can make a difference in the lives of those we love.

Watching, waiting, and hoping do not require a brilliant mind, professional expertise, or strong opinions. They are a form of ministry needed at many times in life. People watch, wait, and hope for opportunities for more education, a job change, increased income, a child to mature, resolution of conflict, healing. When the time is right, they are ready to step in to offer support, direction, or strength to those in need.

We can find many reasons to not be there to wait, watch, and hope. Maybe we are afraid of the outcome so we back away from the potential hurt. Maybe we run out of patience. Maybe we are afraid that we are too flawed to help. Whatever the argument against it, God has a better reason for it: He tells us to wait in hope and trust in Him.

In the Bible, when Jesus was hurting, He asked His disciples to simply stay awake with Him. The failure of the disciples to be there for Jesus, and His subsequent forgiveness, can encourage all of us to simply be there for others in their hour of need. They don't need our perfect words or wisdom. They just need us to watch, wait, and hope with them.

RC

HopePrayer

Lord, I do not have the strength in myself to be there for someone. I really don't. So I ask You to fill me, to show my loved ones Your strength through me, to love them through me. Thank You, Lord.

Personal Sacrifice

HopeWord

> *Do not neglect to do good and to share what you*
> *have, for such sacrifices are pleasing to God.*

HEBREWS 13:16 ESV

HopeMinute

There I was, comfortably planted on our sofa watching some sports game on television. I don't even remember which game it was. All I know is that one of my children asked if I would get them something from the kitchen. I was aghast! They wanted *me* to get up and walk maybe twenty feet?! Just to get them something? (Well, I probably wasn't really aghast, but I sure felt inconvenienced.)

Then my heart was convicted. What a small request. And from someone I love dearly. Getting it was the very least I could do. It was only twenty feet away.

What if someone asked me to do something that involved walking or running a mile? How about more than ten or twenty miles? Wow. Talk about inconvenienced. But that is what many people do to raise money for research, victims, or awareness. They sacrifice time, energy, and in many cases, tolerate pain, for what they believe in.

That is the sort of sacrifice that Jesus expects from us. That "going out of our way to help another" attitude is what God required of His disciples and what He still asks of us. Sacrifice. It is not too much to ask. RC

HopePrayer

Lord, sometimes I'm not terribly sacrificial. Please show me where You would have me sacrifice, what I could do for someone, what sacrifice I could make that would make a difference. After all, You sacrificed everything for me. I ask You to speak to me on this, and make me willing to do whatever You call me to do.

Courtesy

HopeWord

> *Pursue a righteous life—a life of wonder,*
> *faith, love, steadiness, courtesy.*

1 Timothy 6:11 THE MESSAGE

HopeMinute

Courtesy—or the lack of it—sets a first impression that can be as permanent as a handprint in concrete. Isn't it amazing how quickly behavior patterns seem to make an impact on the people? Those who know us well and even those who don't know us at all make judgments about our behavior according to how courteous or discourteous we are.

There are some people I know who are just kind, courteous people. There are others I know who are just not. Our hearts and our self-absorption are revealed when we are inconvenienced. The first thing that goes is usually common courtesy.

Regardless of other strengths and natural giftings, courtesy is a behavior that everyone can develop. It shows respect for others. It shows gratitude. A friendly disposition makes even the most unfair, uncomfortable situations much better. And it costs nothing.

So much grace and kindness have been shown to us. Courtesy is a way of mirroring that to others. If we treat each situation with grace and the people we meet with kindness, we extend the courtesy that our Father has extended to us. On a bad day, courtesy makes all the difference.

RC

HopePrayer

Dear Lord, I ask You to show me where I am not courteous and help me to be courteous. It's as simple as focusing on others instead of on myself. I pray that You heighten my awareness of others and show me strong ways to be courteous. What a blessing courtesy is. I want to bless others that way. Thank You, Lord.

Rest Giver

Come to me, all you who are weary and burdened,
and I will give you rest. Take my yoke upon you
and learn from me, for I am gentle and humble
in heart, and you will find rest for your souls.
For my yoke is easy and my burden is light.

MATTHEW 11:28–30 NIV

HopeMinute

Having a bad day? A bad month? A bad year? Does it feel like you are on the edge and just one more thing will send you over? Perhaps recent news or developments caused you to feel as though you have been written off, forgotten, and hopeless.

I don't know exactly how you feel, but I have felt written off before. I know how painful hopelessness can be. I suppose the journey through "the valley of the shadow of death" (Psalm 23:4) feels like a "journey through hell." The writer of that Psalm was able to make it through because God did not abandon him. The same is true for us: God will not abandon us. He will lead us to peace.

I believe that all of us will experience (sometimes in very mysterious ways) the love of God in the midst of agony and pain. I know that God is for you and not against you. He is our rest-giver. Many of those who have journeyed through hell find rest and refreshment by simply trusting God. With His help our burdens are lighter. Our journey is easier. Our rest is more complete. May God's rest be yours today.   RC

HopePrayer

Well, Lord, it's You and me. I have no power over these overwhelming problems, especially the ones that pile insurmountably high, the ones that feel like a journey through hell. But those are the times I can grow closest to You. I *long* to be close to You. Take my burdens, Lord, and give me rest. Please, I need Your rest.

Surrender

> *Praise be to the Lord, to God our Savior,*
> *who daily bears our burdens.*
>
> PSALM 68:19 NIV

HopeMinute

Perhaps the heaviest burden we try to carry is the burden of mistakes and failures. They make us angry and bitter and ungrateful. It is so hard to know what to do with our failures. How do we live with them?

Even if you've fallen, even if you've failed, even if everyone has rejected you, God will not turn away from you. He came first and foremost to those who have no hope. He goes to those no one else would go to and says, "I'll give you grace and I'll give you eternity."

Only you can let go and surrender your cares and concerns to God. Only He can take those away for you. In order for Him to do so, you must cast your anxieties, worries, problems, fears, and failures on the One who cares for you more than any other.

God is not about guilt and shame. He is about forgiveness and grace. He is also not about trying harder and performing better. He is about resting and becoming more dependent on Him—letting Him live through you. When we have done wrong, we want to be convicted, but when we give those things to God, we are free from guilt and shame.

When we lay down our cares and our mistakes, we are free to experience life as He designed it. It helps us be thankful for the many blessings we all have. Give all your concerns and burdens to Him so you can rest in the fullness of His love and grace. All it takes is surrender.

RC

HopePrayer

God, I am simply exhausted from carrying these mistakes. I lay them at Your feet, and rest in Your love and grace. I surrender.

God Listens

> *I love the Lord because he hears my voice*
> *and my prayer for mercy.*
> *Because he bends down to listen,*
> *I will pray as long as I have breath!*
>
> PSALM 116:1–2 NLT

Did you know that you can talk to God? Just talk to Him like you would talk to your best friend. There are no right words. There is no right way. Just speak. Talk. Laugh. Cry. Scream. He already knows how you feel so go ahead and talk it up.

You can talk to God because God listens. So often when we talk to people, they see us talking but don't really hear us. Your voice matters in heaven. God takes you very seriously. He turns to hear your voice.

There is no need to fear that you will be ignored. Even if you stammer or stumble, even if what you have to say impresses no one else, it impresses God. Moan, groan, and blubber your way through a conversation with Him if you have to. He will understand. He just wants to hear from you.

He listens to your requests, your confessions, your thankfulness. God listens. Intently. Carefully. Just speak.

RC

HopePrayer

Dear Lord, too many times I have been so busy with other things that I have neglected to come talk to You. Or I have felt like such a failure that I am reluctant to come talk to You. Or sometimes my hurt is so deep that I just don't have the words. Lord, I love You. I'm just going to climb in Your lap and sit for a while. I don't have any profound words...so let's just talk.

Sharing in the Suffering

HopeWord

> *Rejoice with those who rejoice,*
> *weep with those who weep.*
>
> ROMANS 12:15 ESV

HopeMinute

Some of us wonder how we will live the rest of our lives with the problems and trials we are currently carrying. The burden is heavy and at times seems unbearable. The days loom long, with no reprieve in sight.

There is great power and relief in formulating new plans and goals for ourselves, our children, and our families. These plans—social, spiritual, academic, volunteer—are especially helpful for us if they revolve around other people, many of whom have greater problems than our own. There is solace in giving to others, especially if we give unasked and from our hearts. Sometimes just crying along with someone is the greatest gift you can give. Both of you feel better.

Sharing this hope that we have, sharing our faith and experiences with others who may be suffering is a caring gesture. But it is also a wonderful opportunity to see ourselves and our problems more clearly. Coming alongside someone, sharing in their suffering, sharing your experiences, will keep you focused on others, and that is always tremendously fulfilling. Then, further down the road, you will have the foundation to look beyond yourself when you are suffering. You may even be able to laugh.

RC

HopePrayer

Lord, please show me what new plans You would like me to make to ease this burden I'm carrying. Show me specific ways to lessen the weight of it. And please, show me how I can help carry someone else's burden. Thank You, Lord.

Rest and Repair

HopeWord

> *The Lord replied, "My Presence will go*
> *with you, and I will give you rest."*
>
> EXODUS 33:14 NIV

HopeMinute

Every once in a while the burdens of life get us down. We just can't bring ourselves to be hopeful and optimistic all the time. The burdens seem to overwhelm us. It's so important to know that we can let go of those burdens for a day or two. We need to allow ourselves to take a much-needed rest.

There will be days when we can find no reason to get out of bed. That's okay. We can take a mental health day by relaxing. We can pamper ourselves every once in a while to repair our resolve and rejuvenate our souls.

Too many of us feel guilty if we give in to our feelings of sadness, disgust, anger, or exhaustion. We think we have to keep a phony, happy face showing all the time. That can certainly take its toll on us emotionally as well as physically. By taking a day to deal with our emotions, to rest and refresh ourselves, we are better able to be optimistic and hopeful the rest of the time. It's not showing weakness, it is taking time to gather strength.

Rest is important. If God felt it was important enough to tell us to rest and to take a day of rest Himself, don't you think we should? RC

HopePrayer

Lord, I do need rest. I cannot continue at this pace without it. Please, give me rest. Give me peace. And rejuvenate me so I'm ready to go on.

A Beautiful Life

> *You should clothe yourselves instead with the beauty*
> *that comes from within, the unfading beauty of a*
> *gentle and quiet spirit, which is so precious to God.*

1 PETER 3:4 NLT

We all have, in our mind's eye, a picture of what life would be like if we were healthy, wealthy, and could do whatever we wanted with our days. If given the choice between health and sickness, wealth and poverty, most people would choose the former of both. We would choose what we think of as "a beautiful life."

Yet, there are no assurances of easy living no matter how healthy or wealthy we are. Howard Hughes struggled mightily at the end of his life with a search to give his life meaning beyond his wealth. There are several Fortune 500 executives going through the same thing right now.

When our wish to "have it easy" becomes a preoc-
cupation, our world can become stressful, unsettling,
and un-peaceful. We spend so much time wishing for
greener pastures that we stop counting our own blessings. That is a mistake. We need to recognize that this
"wish" creates stress that can bring about problems in
every aspect of our lives—emotionally, relationally, and
even physically. But this kind of stress can be avoided.

We need to trust in God's perfect ways and return to
the reality of our own beautiful life. Look around you.
Notice all the blessings. If you start counting them, you
will find there are more than you ever imagined. Family. Friends. Freedom. Sunrises. Chocolate. A parking
space. You have a beautiful life.   RC

HopePrayer

Lord, please move my attention away from the seemingly more appealing lives of others and instead help
me focus on You. Let me not look "without" for beauty
and instead look "within" at You. Show me the beauty
of what I have.

Just Pray

HopeWord

> *Anyone who is having troubles should pray.*
> *Anyone who is happy should sing praises.*

JAMES 5:13 NCV

HopeMinute

Do you want to know how to deepen your prayer life? Pray. Don't prepare to pray. Just pray. Don't read about prayer. Just pray. Don't attend a lecture on prayer or engage in discussion about prayer. Just pray.

Many times I will hear my wife, Susan, talking in the kitchen as she is doing the dishes or making dinner. No one around. Except her and God. She is praying. A wonderful, intimate conversation with God.

Posture, tone, and place are personal matters. Select the form that works for you. But don't think too much about it. There is no right way or wrong way to pray. Don't be so concerned about wrapping the gift that you never give it. Better to pray awkwardly than not at all.

Don't be afraid to pray when you are angry at God either. He already knows your heart. He can take it.

Prayer is not a religious act or ritual. It is just a conversation. So pray. He is listening.

RC

HopePrayer

God, it's just You and me. I have been busy, forgetful, hurt, so I don't feel like praying. But I'm here now, ready for this time. Let me tell You some things that have been on my heart....

Keeping Life Full

> *Just as you accepted*
> *Christ Jesus as your Lord,*
> *you must continue to follow him.*
> *Let your roots grow down into him,*
> *and let your lives be built on him.*
> *Then your faith will grow strong*
> *in the truth you were taught, and*
> *you will overflow with thankfulness.*
>
> COLOSSIANS 2:6–7 NLT

HopeMinute

"The more things you love, the more you are interested in, the more you enjoy, the more you have left when anything happens." Ethel Barrymore's quote reminds me of how important it is to fill our lives with people, hobbies, and interests. And what better time to start than today?

Now is a good time to pursue your interests and to nurture both new and old relationships. Now is a great time for families to rejoice in each other, heal wounds, and love each other as is, unconditionally, as we are loved by God.

We understand how easily and quickly circumstances can change. This understanding nudges us to expand our experiences, to take advantage of each day, each moment. We strive to be slow to anger and quick to forgive. Not one of us is immune to the troubles of life. Whether the trouble is an illness or something else—finances, marital problems, loss of a job—we all suffer at one time or another.

Keeping our lives as full as possible with the love of good people and the challenge of activities provides support even during the most difficult times. When we have other things to focus on, responsibilities to turn to, we find it helps the healing. Tragedies and hard times will find you, but the joy, love, and hope found in the fullness of life are powerful medicines that will help you overcome.

HopePrayer

Lord, will You show me something You have new for me today? I could use a breath of fresh air—a hobby, an interest, or a person You would like me to pursue. Thank You, Lord, for Your mercies that are new every morning and for always doing a new thing!

Choose To Fight

> *Let us not grow weary of doing good, for in due*
> *season we will reap, if we do not give up.*
>
> GALATIANS 6:9 ESV

I have torn ligaments in each of my knees. It is probably due to some fun times with my kids on a trampoline (made worse by a role in our community theater where I had to drop to my knees and crawl around for *several* performances). I have been to an orthopedic surgeon. He wanted to operate but told me that it wouldn't really make much of a difference whether he did or not. He said I would always have problems—that I would develop arthritis in that knee at some point. So, I pretty much gave up.

Then about a year ago, I had a revelation. How could I encourage people with life-threatening illnesses to fight their diseases if I so easily gave up on what I was struggling with? I had no authority. Why should people listen to me? So I began a plan to get in better shape to relieve some of the daily pressure I was putting on my knees.

Weight loss has been a life-long battle for me. It was one of those hurdles I thought I could never overcome. It has been a year since I began to take action. Total weight loss: sixty pounds and counting! I am feeling great. My knees have never felt better.

During the past year, there were many, many times when I was ready to give up. It was just too hard. The progress was too slow. But I replaced those thoughts with determination: I chose not to quit. And I began again each time. Eventually, a feeling of accomplishment settled in.

I know there are times when you want to quit; when fighting doesn't seem worth the pain; when the challenges you face bring thoughts of giving up. Choose to fight. Decide not to let your problems control you. Hold tight to hope and keep try-

ing. Don't give up. If I can do it, you can do it. Keep
fighting. RC

HopePrayer

Lord, You know the areas where I have given up the
fight. Will You please show me which fight is worth
taking up? Strengthen me with resolve, lead the plan,
and renew my hope! I don't want to roll over and play
dead—I want to fight until the end! Thank You, Lord.

The Gift of Love

HopeWord

> *For everything we know about God's Word is*
> *summed up in a single sentence: Love others as you*
> *love yourself. That's an act of true freedom.*
>
> GALATIANS 5:14 THE MESSAGE

HopeMinute

No matter what happens to us in our lifetime, regardless of whether we are rich or poor, strong or weak, ill or well, we always have room for love. Unqualified love and caring cost nothing and pay invaluable dividends. Despite our financial position, allowing ourselves to love, allowing ourselves to be loved, strengthens and lends greater value to our lives. Loving helps restore hope to even the most uncertain future. It transforms our lives and gives us meaning.

In loving others and in being loved, we are reminded that people, not events or even characteristics, are the important elements of our lives. We don't look for perfection in our loved ones and they aren't looking for it in us. We need to free ourselves of the notion that we must earn love. Love is a gift, not a dividend. It comes freely from others and from God.

Love is the great equalizer: we can all give and receive it. You don't have to be rich, smart, healthy, wise, or even nice. It is free for all. Take time today to express your love for others and to accept their love for you. It is a choice you'll be glad you made. RC

HopePrayer

God, You loved me first. Thank You! Now, please help me love others as You've loved me. Help me focus on others and love them without requiring anything in return.

Disasters

> *But now the Lord my God has given me rest on*
> *every side, and there is no adversary or disaster.*
>
> 1 KINGS 5:4 NIV

HopeMinute

Do you remember the "disastrous" events of your childhood? Not having the right Halloween costume, failing a math test, not having a date for the prom? They seem of little importance now. Most are probably even humorous memories.

The vast majority of things we worry about today never do happen. But the damage from the stress may already be done. The Bible tells us to "be anxious for nothing." Understanding that we worry too much and that many events have only a brief importance helps us view our current problems more realistically.

Financial difficulties, family dissension, or an accelerating disease are all very serious and require our attention or adjustment. But we deal with these problems better if we remember that very few problems are really disastrous. They are inconvenient or even painful, but our lives can accommodate them. We go on.

Acknowledging that most problems are not catastrophic will reduce the stress and lessen the negative physical and emotional impact that comes from worrying, being anxious, and overreacting.

Remember that God is indeed bigger than anything we face. He promises that, with Him, we will not go through anything too big to handle. God is in control. He will get us through the situation, even if it does turn out to be a disaster.

RC

HopePrayer

Lord, thank You for being in control of everything in my life. Please give me perspective on my problems, show me how temporary most of them are, and bring the answers You want me to have.

Never Mind

> *Blessed be God,*
> *Who has not turned away my prayer,*
> *Nor His mercy from me!*
>
> PSALM 66:20 NKJV

HopeMinute

Bob circled the parking lot again. He had an important meeting and couldn't find a parking place. He could not afford to be late. He was really sweating now. Looking up toward heaven, he said, "God, take pity on me. If You find me a parking place I will go to church every Sunday for the rest of my life and give up drinking!" Miraculously, a parking place appeared. Bob looked up again and said, "Never mind. I found one."

It is usually in the midst of our most desperate situations when many people turn to God for help. No doubt you have probably turned to God yourself and prayed for Him to intervene. Maybe you've even begged Him for some miraculous cure or specific knowledge.

It's one thing to turn to God in prayer, but quite another to deal with answers you don't like. How do you respond to the way God answers your prayers? Are you like Bob when he miraculously found a parking place? Or do you recognize His answers and give thanks to God in all things and for all things?

God loves each and every one of us unconditionally. He wants us to turn to Him in every situation, not just when things seem desperate and out of our control. We don't always recognize His answers for what they are, but we need to thank Him anyway. He is always looking out for us, always providing for us.   JT

HopePrayer

Well, Lord, I have to laugh! I'm thinking of times I thought I was so smart, or so talented, but it was You all along! I repent of the many times—a day—that You "found my parking space" and I didn't realize it was You. Show me, Lord, Your continual and miraculous presence.

Tomorrow

> *Therefore do not be anxious about tomorrow,*
> *for tomorrow will be anxious for itself.*
> *Sufficient for the day is its own trouble.*

MATTHEW 6:34 ESV

HopeMinute

How are we to prepare for tomorrow when God only promises us today? We don't know what's ahead of us. But God knows. He doesn't always show us what's in store for us or even if we will have a tomorrow. So how do we go forward?

We prepare for what might come by growing in our faith. Part of that growth comes by living our lives as if each day is the last. By taking advantage of opportunities to tell our children, spouse, family, and friends how much we love and appreciate them. By doing what needs to be done today while preparing ourselves for eternity.

Whatever your beliefs are, my prayer is the same: may God reveal the truth to you and may you come to know Him more. I also pray that you come to live by faith so that whatever tomorrow brings you will be ready for it.

If we give tomorrow to God and concentrate on today, we can enjoy this day for the wonderful gift it is. And it can be wonderful. Enjoy! RC

HopePrayer

Lord, please remind me that whatever I'm doing is happening today. Focus me, direct me, and help me to live each day to the fullest, and to be grateful for the blessing that is today. Help me release my tomorrow to You.

Making Mistakes

> *If you, O Lord, kept a record of sins, O Lord,*
> *who could stand? But with you there is forgiveness;*
> *therefore you are feared. I wait for the Lord,*
> *my soul waits, and in his word I put my hope.*

PSALM 130:3–5 NIV

HopeMinute

Once a long time ago, I made a mistake. And then another, and another, and another, and another. You get the idea. I make them all the time. Mistakes are not the issue. It is what we do with mistakes and what we learn from them that matter.

I have made a tearful plea many times, "God, show me what to do. I just don't want to make a mistake."

If our children were intent on avoiding mistakes, they would never take their first stumbling step or speak their first babbling word. They would quit writing after their first spelling test and quit playing games after their first recess. How wonderful that our children do not immediately acquire a fear of failure. They instinctively view life as a journey. Maybe we need to get back to those instincts.

As adults, we tend to view life—and even faith—as a performance. Someone might be keeping score so we better try really hard. I get exhausted just writing that. What a terrible way to live. Living like that magnifies mistakes and diminishes the significance of our daily journey.

The focus of performance is perfection. The focus of a journey, however, is direction. Mistakes can be wise teachers if we let God speak to us through them. The correction refines our direction. Instead of trying harder, just relax and learn to follow God's voice. He will direct your steps.

RC

HopePrayer

God, show me what to do. I just want to hear Your voice and take the next step. Let me seek direction, not perfection. Thank You, Lord.

Unshakeable Faith

The Lord says, "My thoughts are not like your thoughts.
Your ways are not like my ways.
Just as the heavens are higher than the earth,
so are my ways higher than your ways
and my thoughts higher than your thoughts."

ISAIAH 55:8–9 NCV

HopeMinute

When a crisis occurs—bad test results, a job loss, an accident—many of us pass through the "why me?" phase. We may become confused and feel we have been personally selected for bad times. Our faith may be shaken. God is okay with that.

Don't be afraid to tell God you are disappointed with Him or angry at Him. He already knows your heart. It can take us a while to recognize that we still do have a strong, abiding faith. Time passes and we come to understand that His ways are not always our ways, but He loves us and always does what is best for us, even when we cannot fathom why or how.

His timing is not always our timing. He can see things we cannot and His timing is always perfect. We come to understand that sometimes the answers are not easy, but our faith has carried us through the difficult time. Our belief in a God greater than ourselves takes hold, rather firmly, until we feel an even stronger sense of faith and purpose than before.

Martin Luther wrote, "Faith is living an unshakeable confidence, a belief in the grace of God so assured that a man would die a thousand deaths for its sake." Sometimes we don't recognize it for what it is, but God has placed in us a foundation of faith that will hold up in the face of tragedy. It is okay to question. It is okay to be angry. When the dust settles, our faith will still see us through.

RC

HopePrayer

God, thank You that You have given me Your faith, faith I am incapable of producing. Lord, I am shaken: I do need Your help. Please hold me close while the dust swirls around me, and once it settles, I want to be standing on faith.

Love Is an Action

> *For I am sure that neither death nor life, nor angels*
> *nor rulers, nor things present nor things to come,*
> *nor powers, nor height nor depth, nor anything else*
> *in all creation, will be able to separate us from the*
> *love of God in Christ Jesus our Lord.*
>
> ROMANS 8:38–39 ESV

HopeMinute

The greatest love story ever told is found in the Bible.
The story is about how God loves us unconditionally,
as we are. His grace and love are available to us fully
and completely. No red tape. It is a free gift available to
anyone who is willing to receive it.

In response to receiving that gift, we are asked
to walk in love. "Love the Lord with all your heart,
with all your soul, and with all your mind." Also,
"love your neighbor as yourself" (from Matthew

22:37–38). That sounds great. But how in the world do we do that?

The bad news is: we can't. The good news is: He can. All He asks of us is to allow Him to love others through us. We come to know Him and His love better by spending time with Him, by reading the Bible, by prayer, by just getting to know Him better.

Love is not just an emotion or a mushy feeling. Love is an action. The Bible gives us a list of what love looks like: it is patient and kind; it does not envy; it is not puffed up; it does not behave rudely; it is not self focused; it is not easily provoked; it rejoices in the truth; it bears all things, believes all things, hopes all things, endures all things; love never fails (from 1 Corinthians 13).

The Bible also says that God is love. God never fails. In His plan for your life, in His love and grace for you, in His teaching more about Himself, He is always right and true. We can never fail as we walk in that kind of love. It is the unconditional, unselfish love of God. As we abide in Him and let His Word abide in us, our joy will be full. RC

HopePrayer

God, I think I missed it somewhere about understanding unconditional love. Would You please start over with me? Like an algebra problem I didn't understand, start at the beginning. Just show me how fully You love me.

LOL

He will yet fill your mouth with laughter
and your lips with shouts of joy.

JOB 8:21 NIV

HopeMinute

Part of working with HopeKids requires a willingness to be a clown, to just let down your guard, get goofy, and have fun with the kids. It is probably one of the things I enjoy most about my involvement. It's the fun part.

A sense of humor is an essential tool in life. Unfortunately, it is most difficult to keep when we're under stress—the time when we need it the most. I find it difficult to laugh and keep my eyes focused where they should be when I am worried or the day is trying. In the face of a crisis, we often find ourselves irritable and in a bad mood, even if we know, deep in our hearts, that such an attitude is not in our best interest.

Making the choice between bitterness and acceptance is easier when we take ourselves less seriously. Finding the funny side of life helps us deal with the most difficult situations life has to offer. Humor cleanses us through laughter. It is wonderfully healing. It draws others to us and bonds us. It brightens your life and the lives of others.

So, go ahead, laugh out loud.

RC

HopePrayer

Remind me to laugh, Lord, at the things my kids say or just the idea of a duck-billed platypus. Show me the humor where I don't see it. Show me Your mirth and let me join in it.

Perfect Timing

> *Now may the Lord direct your hearts into the love*
> *of God and into the patience of Christ.*

2 THESSALONIANS 3:5 NKJV

HopeMinute

I am not the most patient guy. I am just now coming to learn the depth of God's perfect timing and provision. I've come to accept that God has a plan. The details of exactly what will happen and when are without flaw. But what is my role in all of this? I'm learning that it is to simply have patience, listen for His voice, and follow. To be completely honest, sometimes the results that I seek don't happen as quickly as I would like.

Have you ever heard of the bamboo in Japan that only blossoms once every 120 years? No one knows how this plant can keep track of time, but we do know that how it's cared for during the 119 years before it germinates will determine how much the bamboo will bloom in the following year. That's a long time to wait to see the results. The people who care for the plant in the beginning won't be around to see the glory of the bloom. Their care, however, will affect what others see.

In the same way, life doesn't always blossom on our timetable. The healing of our children, the healing of a marriage, the resolution of personal issues sometimes don't come as fast as we would like. The healing is often not scripted as you would have written it. That is very, very hard.

The faith you have in God's perfect love and timing, your belief and trust in Him should not waiver just because results aren't immediate. Be patient. The late blooms often have the most striking and beautiful flowers.

RC

HopePrayer

Lord, I need Your patience. Show me the beauty of what's ahead. Help me wait for You. Thank You, Lord.

Overcoming Limitations

> *I have said these things to you, that in me you may*
> *have peace. In the world you will have tribulation.*
> *But take heart; I have overcome the world.*

JOHN 16:33 ESV

HopeMinute

You have so much to offer. You are more of a blessing to more people than you can ever imagine. I know it is hard to see that, especially when circumstances in life seem to overwhelm us. But it is true.

There are some circumstances we cannot change or control. One of those is certainly the limiting nature of illness. Disease, treatments, and side effects have a huge impact on life. But you are not required to deal with these things alone.

It may not be the same as something like cancer, but all people have to deal with handicaps or limita-

84

tions—physical, psychological, or emotional. People dealing with life-changing issues are challenged to live a fulfilling life within the limitations placed upon them. What matters most is that even though you may be dealing with a long-term problem, you can learn to dwell on wellness, not on illness; on solutions, not problems. You can be productive, supportive, inventive, creative—in spite of limitations.

The key is to lift our eyes to something greater, to Someone greater. Limitations can certainly affect how we live each day, but they need not alter who we are or the quality of our lives. It is our choice. Life has so much to offer us and we have so much to offer life. Don't limit yourself. Live. Hope. Bless others.   RC

HopePrayer

Lord, I ask You to show me that You are unlimited! I cannot do all that I want, but You can! Please, Lord, reveal the blessings You have put in me and speak through me to bless others.

Sweet Sorrow

HopeWord

> *Sorrow is better than laughter,*
> *For by a sad countenance the heart is made better.*
>
> ECCLESIASTES 7:3 NKJV

HopeMinute

If I had to choose extreme happiness or extreme sorrow, I think I would choose extreme sorrow.

During a time of extreme, overwhelming happiness, our thoughts stray. We often forget God, His provision and blessings. Our faith, our trust, seem to become less vital to our daily walk. Things that are truly important in life become overshadowed by temporal and temporary pleasures. And usually when this time passes, we can become bitter and angry instead of grateful.

During a time of extreme sorrow, however, our thoughts are much more spiritual. When we get to the end of ourselves and have no answers, we turn to God.

Our faith and our trust deepen. Only when our shoulders cannot bear the load do we finally place the burden on His very capable shoulders. When this time of sorrow passes, and it will, our hearts are filled with thankfulness.

I know many of you are in that place right now. You are in a time of overwhelming sorrow and confusion and fear. This can indeed become a time of tremendous blessing and growth for you and your family. God is there and He will always answer. Always. Sometimes the answer is yes, sometimes no, sometimes wait, and sometimes He just says that His grace is sufficient to get you through. And it is.

RC

HopePrayer

Lord, I'm not sure I dare ask for extreme sorrow... but I do ask that You keep my mind focused on You. My shoulders can't carry those heavy burdens, so I ask that You lift them and put them on Yours.

Beauty Is Truth

All you nations, praise the Lord.
All you people, praise him
because the Lord loves us very much,
and his truth is everlasting.
Praise the Lord!

PSALM 117:1–2 NCV

HopeMinute

I heard Michael W. Smith in concert recently, playing songs with a symphony orchestra. I marveled at the profound beauty of the music, and remembered the quote by George Keats, "Beauty is truth, truth beauty, that is all I know on earth and all I need to know." And I wondered: what makes this concert beautiful, while random notes played by children on the same instruments would be hard on the ears? What is the difference?

The world tries to teach us these days that there are no absolutes, that "what's good for me is all that matters." But my experience does not bear that out. Sure, we have a wide variety of tastes (I may prefer jazz and you may prefer country music), but generally, flowers are beautiful and a barren expanse of dirt is not; vanilla smells lovely and a sewer does not.

Our post-modern culture may say that there are no absolute truths, but that is not so. Some things are beautiful and some just aren't, even allowing for individual tastes. The world is not that random: there are some universal truths. When we begin to follow the common thread, it leads us to intelligent design in our world. To live as though there are no universal truths is to have to rethink every aspect of life from scratch, to reinvent truth with every new question. Intelligent design—planned, plotted, purposeful life—leads us to God's truth. And that is beautiful.

Seeing beauty as truth and truth as beauty allows me to appreciate the design God has put into this world. It is that common experience of beauty that allows one group of musicians to make music that thousands of people will enjoy. It is that experience that allows us to recognize and praise God as the one true, beautiful God.

SC

HopePrayer

You are so beautiful, Lord, and You created in us a longing for beauty. Fill me Lord, I pray, with Your truth and Your beauty....

A Mindset for Miracles

> *God, we thank you;*
> *we thank you because you are near.*
> *We tell about the miracles you do.*
> *You say, "I set the time for trial,*
> *and I will judge fairly.*
> *The earth with all its people may shake,*
> *but I am the one who holds it steady."*

PSALM 75:1-3 NCV

HopeMinute

In some houses of worship, it is not politically correct to talk about God performing miracles, much less expect Him to perform them. The Old and New Testaments, however, are packed with the miraculous. Take, for example, the time Paul was bitten by a snake. He just shook the snake off into the fire and "suffered no ill effects." I believe that actually happened. The poison was real and the people around him expected him to swell up and die.

Paul, evidently, had a different mindset. The life-threatening reality was apparently meaningless to Paul. I am not sure what he had that we do not. Maybe it was that he didn't live in a culture that places its trust in science. We know he had an unshakable trust and faith in God and we know he had a strong purpose in life. Maybe he just wouldn't let himself be sidetracked by anything, not even poison from a snake bite.

Every day I realize more and more how attitude is critical when we are battling life-threatening illnesses or life-changing challenges. I believe it plays a far bigger role in healing than we realize. I have seen miracles and I have heard about many more: tumors suddenly disappear, jobs appear out of nowhere, money issues are resolved, long-held grudges dissolve.

If it is a miracle you need, start by believing that a miracle is possible in your life. I have seen and heard too much not to encourage you to believe in God's power and in what He might do. The Bible is full of examples of God's healing. He healed the broken-hearted, the sick, the sinners, the land, nations, and even water. He is steady when we are shaky. He is constant when we are unsure. He is miraculous.

Do you believe in miracles? Do you expect them? What do you need to do to cultivate a miracle mindset? When thinking about your challenges, leave room for the possibility of miracles. RC

HopePrayer

Lord, I need a miracle. I do believe in miracles; help me in my unbelief. I pray for Your specific miracle for my situation. Thank You, Lord.

Freedom From Negativity

> *Trust in the Lord and do good; dwell in the land and*
> *enjoy safe pasture. Delight yourself in the Lord and*
> *he will give you the desires of your heart. Commit your*
> *way to the Lord; trust in him and he will do this.*
>
> PSALM 37:3–5 NIV

HopeMinute

Some people wonder whether or not God wants us to be well. Do you? Instead of getting into a big religious discussion, let me appeal to your common sense. God created us, didn't He? Are we not then valuable? Are we not worthy of love, if for no other reason than we were created by God, whose very essence is love?

I understand why you might wonder, though. It's the pain and suffering. It's the sicknesses. It's the feeling of powerlessness. It is a tinge of anger and frustration about how the whole situation is impacting your whole family.

I cannot move you from anger to gladness or from frustration to bliss. I can't do anything for you now except to remind you of the truth, and I can only trust that the truth will set you free from any negativity you are feeling. Consider this: Thousands upon thousands have gone through what you are going through. Many have been considerably more sick or in bigger trouble and have gone on to reclaim health and wholeness again.

It's going to be all right. Healing does come. Always. Just not always in our timing or ways. Focus on God's unconditional love for you and your family. Trust Him and His ways. He will get you through whatever the future holds.

RC

HopePrayer

Dear Lord, I pray for Your complete healing. Please heal the sickness or trouble. But also I ask you to heal my pain, my anger, my doubt. You said that I could know the truth and the truth would set me free. Lord, please set me free with Your truth.

A Note of Encouragement

> *Therefore encourage one another and build*
> *each other up, just as in fact you are doing.*

1 THESSALONIANS 5:11 NIV

HopeMinute

Want to do something for your family that they will never forget? Write them a meaningful note. It's not to be instructional. Don't correct. Don't teach. We do that enough. In fact, there is probably nothing you could say that they haven't heard before. Many times. This is something very different.

It's a note of encouragement—from your heart to theirs. Why a written note? In this day of instant messages and e-mail, written notes mean more than ever. Your family will read it and absorb it without interruptions. They'll receive it without pressure. Without having to think about how to respond.

Include three things in the note. First, let them know that you love them for who they are. Second, describe and praise them for their unique talents, gifts and abilities. Third, tell them what you want them to remember about your relationship.

Speak a blessing into the life of your family. Don't worry about having the perfect words. Just share your heart. They will remember and treasure it forever. RC

HopePrayer

Lord, I am so good at correcting my family, instructing my family, telling my family what to do. Now, would You please help me simply encourage them? Help me write a love note for my family. Help me see my family as You see them, and then be able to write that in a note.

Unnecessary Unhappiness

HopeWord

> When Jesus saw him lying there and learned
> that he had been in this condition for a long time,
> he asked him, "Do you want to get well?"
>
> JOHN 5:6 NIV

HopeMinute

Many people complain about life's problems, but few actually get around to doing much about them. It is our nature to complain. That is why suggestion boxes don't work. People fill them with complaints instead of solutions.

Most of us have never been taught basic problem-solving skills. We find ourselves being unnecessarily unhappy. When we are unhappy, we need to ask the question, "What do I want in order for the unhappiness to go away?" Sometimes we come up with good solutions. Often, we have no idea what to do. If what we want

98

cannot be accomplished, then our anxiety and complaining only serve to frustrate us, and those around us.

When we get to this point we have to adjust our expectations. For example, we may be sad because our child has to go into the hospital. Yet, being in the hospital is exactly the right decision. The treatment our child is receiving is the best course of action.

Someone once wisely said that accepting our limitations makes our future limitless. Adjust your expectations to the reality of your current situation. Accept the options. Improve them if possible.

So, what do you want? Be clear. Communicate it to those who can help you obtain it. If what you want is unobtainable, ask God to help you adjust to a new, more obtainable reality. It will bring about a much happier future. It will restore your hope in the situation. RC

HopePrayer

Lord, I ask You to give me Your perspective. Show me what part of my circumstances, if any, I can change. Then show me what I need to do to accept the rest.

Fear and Faith

God is our refuge and strength, a very present help in trouble.
Therefore we will not fear though the earth gives way,
though the mountains be moved into the heart of the sea.

PSALM 46:1–2 ESV

HopeMinute

It is not the measure of one's faith that is important. What is important is that we give God the measure we have and watch what He can do with it. Just like the parable of the loaves and the fish, if we are willing to give Him what we have, He will take it, bless it, break it, and multiply it into something amazing.

The experience of going through a life-threatening disease with my daughter has reminded me of a few key lessons on fear and faith:

› Fear is alive and well, prowling everywhere it can to steal our joy and our peace.

> Fear and faith cannot occupy the same spirit—one or the other will dominate and take over.
> Fear has only one natural enemy and that is faith.
> The one you feed will grow; the one you starve will die.
> Both fear and faith are contagious and will spread to those around you.
> Both fear and faith grow like the ripples from a pebble dropped in the still water.
> Fear is born of the enemy; faith is the very fruit of God's spirit.
> Fear screams and faith whispers.

I find myself thanking Him for bringing cancer into our lives—it has changed us forever. We will never be the same—we have seen the Lord up close and personal. He is my refuge and my fortress.   JO

HopePrayer

Lord, thank You that faith conquers fear! Remind me to focus on Your faith in me instead of the fear that threatens me. I can't focus on both—I choose faith.

A Positive Revolution

My purpose is that they may be encouraged in heart
and united in love, so that they may have the full
riches of complete understanding, in order that they
may know the mystery of God, namely, Christ.

COLOSSIANS 2:2 NIV

HopeMinute

Affirmation. Praise. Celebration. All of these are
important factors to ensure a positive environment.
We all need those little pats on the back. We appreciate the boost to our spirits that a note or word of praise
gives. We enjoy the warm feeling we get when we cel-
ebrate each other's successes.

It takes only one person to start a positive revolution. Susan and I have found that when the kids are
discouraging to each other, we have also been discouraging. The more positive, loving, and affirming I am to

102

those around me, the more they reflect those attitudes with each other. It only takes one of us to get it started.

Too often, we only notice what others do wrong. We need to notice what they do right! Say thank you for even the smallest things. Give compliments and praise freely and specifically. You might be surprised at how easy it is to improve the overall atmosphere of your home or workplace. You can be the first. You can be the one to start a revolution. Who knows, you might even find some of that appreciation and encouragement coming back to bless you.

RC

HopePrayer

Lord, show me what I can do to praise others. Please adjust my attitude to be more appreciative and less condemning. Let me see others—and speak to them—more positively, the way You see us. Help me to appreciate the little things they do.

One Person at a Time

> *Praise be to the God and Father of our Lord Jesus*
> *Christ, the Father of compassion and the God of*
> *all comfort, who comforts us in all our troubles, so*
> *that we can comfort those in any trouble with the*
> *comfort we ourselves have received form God.*

2 CORINTHIANS 1:3–4 NIV

HopeMinute

I sometimes lose sleep over the pain people are in, the tough situations, the sickness and death in the news and in every day life. The unpredictability—no, the injustice of it all bothers me the most. I want to fix it all—I really do. But if the greatest hearts and minds in the world cannot change the world, cannot solve all the problems as a whole, what can I do?

Jesus, when He walked the earth, grieved about the seemingly unbearable tragedy all around Him. When

His friend Lazarus died, Jesus wept not just because Lazarus was dead, but because of the grief He saw all around Him. The Bible tells us several times that Jesus was moved to compassion for those around Him who were like sheep without a shepherd.

Yet, Jesus healed people who came to Him. He filled the hearts of those who sought Him out. He did not heal the world as a whole, but He offered life to people who came to Him one by one.

As much as my heart is moved, I can't worry about the whole world. I certainly can't fix it. But how about the person near me? To that person I can extend love, grace, and kindness. To my own children? To them I can offer hugs and encouragement. Mother Theresa said, "Never worry about numbers. Help one person at a time, and always start with the person nearest you." That sounds like great advice to me. That is what she did. That is what Jesus did—and what He continues to do. I can't solve all the world's problems, but I can help one person. And that is something I can do right where I am.

HopePrayer.

Dear Lord, will You show me to whom I can reach out and make a difference? Even a small difference? I'm still not quite sure why all this suffering exists, but I ask You to reach out through me to the person nearest me.

The Psalms

> *Be my rock of refuge,*
> *to which I can always go;*
> *give the command to save me,*
> *for you are my rock and my fortress.*

PSALM 71:3 NIV

HopeMinute

Whenever trials and brokenness enter our lives, we look for resources to guide and sustain us through our time of pain. The Book of Psalms is a great source of strength and hope. The Psalms cover a wide range of subjects, both joyful and sorrowful. The book has been used by people of many faiths through many centuries.

The writers appear to experience and reflect on the total experience of life. It's a book for people living in the extremes. Some of the Psalms are dark and angry. Others reflect hope, optimism, and trust. The writers express feelings that God is already aware of, yet they often articulate deep feelings that perhaps we cannot. In the process of reading the Psalms, we can recognize our own soul's cry for help. We can also recognize God's ability to answer our cry.

Certain images from Psalms become particularly helpful during dark times. See how the writer pictures God in Psalm 71:3. Note the images of a strong God: rock, refuge, fortress. These are not words for normal times. In ordinary times, we may prefer to picture God as loving, kind, and tenderhearted. But this text uses war words. They call us to battle. A rock becomes a firm foundation upon which to stand. A fortress surrounds and protects us when we are assaulted by the world. A refuge hides us when evil is pursuing.

God has been protecting mankind since the beginning of time. There is nothing we are going through that He hasn't already dealt with. The Book of Psalms lives as a testament to how God fights for us and protects us from evil. It is very comforting. Have you read it? Today is a good day to start.   RC

HopePrayer

Lord, I find great comfort in the myriad of emotions recorded in the Psalms. My emotions, pleasant or unpleasant, never surprise You. Show me my own heart, and give me courage to express it to You. Thank You, Lord.

Sticks and Stones

> *Gracious words*
> *are like a honeycomb,*
> *sweetness to the soul and*
> *health to the body.*
>
> Proverbs 16:24 esv

HopeMinute

Dr. James Dobson tells a story of when he was in school and all the kids were making fun of one boy's big ears. The kids were all laughing, including Dobson, at this big joke. Suddenly the boy got up and ran out of class *and he never came back*. Dobson couldn't believe it. He said he had no idea that they were offending the kid, and of course he was terribly sorry about it, but it was too late.

Words are something we can never take back. They have a huge impact, especially on children. Negative humor is common, we almost default to it. The "victim" usually goes along with it, rather than revealing how hurt he is. But no one really enjoys it.

It is my prayer that we guard our tongues when angry and even when we are "just teasing." The damage can be greater and last longer than we think. I also hope and pray that we use our words to affirm, convey love, and strengthen others' hearts. The power and impact can be greater and last longer than we can imagine.

If the old rhyme were rewritten to reflect the truth, it would say: "Sticks and stones may break my bones, but words can hurt forever." However, they can also heal and bring hope. They can affirm and comfort. They are powerful. Use them wisely.

SC

HopePrayer

Lord, please remind me today of the power of words. Heal my wounds from careless words said to me, and use my words to bring sweetness and health, not pain. Thank You for Your life-giving words to me.

There Is Hope. Always.

HopeWord

Hope deferred makes the heart sick.

PROVERBS 13:12 NIV

HopeMinute

I cannot imagine how devastating it must be to have a doctor tell you that you or your child only has two months to live. Hope must evaporate like water on a hot Phoenix sidewalk. Unfortunately, this kind of diagnosis happens too often.

Recently, I read a story of an elderly man who was attending a Bible study. He had Alzheimer's. His wife faithfully took him to the study every week, but he just sat there and listened. He hadn't said a word for three whole years. One night the leader shared the story of a doctor who had told his patient that there was no hope, that she had only a month to live. At that moment, the elderly man with Alzheimer's suddenly blurted out, "Tell him to go to hell!" The group was surprised into laughter. They laughed because of the retort and the language the quiet man used was so unexpected. And yet, the words he spoke were the very words the leader was thinking: Tell him to go to hell.

You see, God alone has numbered our days. Only He knows how long we have to live. Let me say that again: *Only He knows how long we have to live.* Not the doctors or anyone else.

Hope deferred not only makes the heart sick, it makes the rest of the body sick as well. Wherever there is life, there is hope. I cannot promise that life will be measured in years. Perhaps it will be measured in decades. Perhaps in months or weeks. But they are *our* months, days, weeks, or years. They do not belong to the doctors.

They belong to us and there is hope. Always.   RC

HopePrayer

Oh Lord, thank You for numbering my days, and the days of my loved ones! I can rest and take heart in that. Remind me to rest in You and to trust You.

Never Stop Dreaming

HopeWord

> *God can do anything, you know—far more*
> *than you could ever imagine or guess or request*
> *in your wildest dreams! He does it not*
> *by pushing us around but by working within us,*
> *his Spirit deeply and gently within us.*

EPHESIANS 3:20–21 THE MESSAGE

HopeMinute

Even as we approach adulthood, we cling to the dreams we had as children. I was going to be a rock star or an actor on the stage. In those days it may have seemed to us that anything was possible. The world was ours for the taking.

It's not immature to hold on to a dream, even when we know the dream may not come true. Mark Twain said, "Don't part with your illusions. When they are gone, you may still exist, but you have ceased to live."

Sometimes I wish for a full head of hair. (Sometimes.) Some of us wish we still had young skin. Some wish for different jobs, athletic abilities, or good health. It is okay to dream those dreams. They refresh our creativity and energy and make us smile.

Our dreams are as important to a healthy, happy future as eating right or exercising. Dreams are essential for hope. Hold dearly to your dreams. Believe. Hope. The possibility of what might occur keeps our days full of wonder and excitement.

RC

HopePrayer

God, the author of hope, remind me of my dreams. Revive in me the dreams I have lost sight of, and bring into being the dreams You want for me. Thank You, Lord, that nothing is impossible for You.

Memories

HopeWord

> *I thank my God every time I remember you. In all*
> *my prayers for all of you, I always pray with joy.*

PHILIPPIANS 1:3–4 NIV

HopeMinute

Before you dig out your old yearbook and start telling "in the good old days" stories about yourself, consider a change of course. Instead, get out videos and photos of your family. Make it an event. Pop some popcorn, gather everyone together, and go back in time. Pass around photos, watch those videos, and talk about the cute and special things your family did when they were younger.

If you can, focus on one person at a time or have a special viewing night for each. Looking back at those days can remind us of our love and compassion for each other, and can even help bring into focus the vision for our future.

It is critical that we help restore laughter and joy to the lives of our families. Keeping them looking forward to the days ahead brings excitement and hope. At the same time, however, it is important that we remember the past and recognize everyone's role in it. Sharing our memories reminds us of what connects us, what makes us a family. It is a very good thing. RC

HopePrayer

Oh, how much we take for granted in our lives! Lord, I thank You for my loved ones, my beautiful family, my friends. Help me to show them, specifically, how precious and special they are. Thank You, Lord.

Hope Worth Waiting For

HopeWord

> *But as for me, I watch in hope for the Lord,*
> *I wait for God my Savior; my God will hear me.*
>
> MICAH 7:7 NIV

HopeMinute

What are we willing to wait for? For children, most of their waiting and hoping is short-term. They wait for the holidays. They wait for the newest toy or the next movie event. They hope that their parents don't find out who made the stain on the carpet. As adults, our waiting more often involves long-term hopes. We hope for good colleges and spouses for our kids. We wait for an enjoyable retirement. We hope for good health.

When you add a critical illness to life, we become masters at the art of waiting and hoping. Waiting to see if the treatment works. Waiting on MRI results.

Hoping for a remission or cure. Hoping for a good day.

The amazing thing is that when we simply wait and hope, we find ourselves losing our self-dependence and increasing our dependence on God and others. That is a good thing. That is as it should be. When we look to God, we look less and less inside ourselves. We trust Him more and more.

Wait, hope, and trust in God's perfect plan and timing. With deepened faith, you will discover a sense of inner peace. And that is something worth waiting and hoping for.

RC

HopePrayer

Waiting...seems to take a lifetime. And I am so impatient. Lord, as You call me to wait and hope, please deepen my patience to do just that. Calm me and give me peace to wait and hope.

My Normal

> *Pray continually; give thanks in all circumstances,*
> *for this is God's will for you in Christ Jesus.*
>
> 1 THESSALONIANS 5:17–18 NIV

Our friends visited from Honduras where they had moved two years ago. I asked the daughter what was different about living there and being back in Arizona. "It is so dry here," she said. "I'm dry all the way down to my stomach! People always said it was dry here, and I thought, yeah, it's dry—it's not wet. But now that I live in a rain forest where it rains all the time, I know what they mean!"

Funny, I thought that "normal" is only what we know. And when it's all we know, it is pretty much the only option. Only when we are out of our normal situation do we see that it was only one of many options.

There are many other "normal" climates all around the world—constant rain, arctic cold, hot and muggy, dry as a bone. Glimpsing other "normals" puts our "normal" into perspective.

When you are consumed with demands—hospitals, money, pain, fighting, struggle, work—that demanding life becomes your "normal." It's hard to remember that other "normals" exist. And though it feels like this life has gone on, and will go on, forever, that's not true. That's why it is important to go someplace fun, to have a date with your spouse, or to visit a friend who is not going through this—anything to try to get a little window into a different "normal."

Life does exist outside of the present demands. It can be a terrible struggle. And when you're in this "normal," you do what you have to do to survive. When you live in Phoenix you drink a lot of water. When you live in Seattle you carry an umbrella.

Trying to grasp another normal viewpoint is healthy and encouraging. It can remind you that life will not always be this way.

SC

HopePrayer

Lord, please show me life outside my own normal. Please give me a broader perspective and help me see things more clearly. Show me that life exists outside of these current circumstances.

The Best Place to Be

> *To everything there is a season,*
> *A time for every purpose under heaven:*
> *A time to be born,*
> *And a time to die...*
> *A time to weep,*
> *And a time to laugh;*
> *A time to mourn,*
> *And a time to dance.*
>
> ECCLESIASTES 3:1–2, 4 NKJV

HopeMinute

I recently celebrated my fiftieth birthday. It seems that as every decade passes, I realize how little I knew in the decade before! Life is better now than it has ever been and I expect that trend to continue. I am already looking forward to my next big birthday!

As I look back on my life, I see that each stage of life

brings its own gifts. When we were young, many of us thought we could conquer the world and that nothing could hurt us. We had the gift of invincibility. We thought we could change people and through them the world. Later, in another stage, the gift is the knowledge that we can really only change ourselves. But through changing ourselves, we finally receive the gift of making a difference.

I do like getting older. The wisdom that comes with age and experience is very comforting to me. As we age, we are better able to accept that whatever stage we are in right now is the perfect place to be. We finally accept that there are things we cannot change and learn to live with that. Time itself alters us.

The time we have lived has created change and impact on the world around us—more than we can imagine. By embracing today, by enjoying the stage of life we are in right now, we bring hope and happiness to those around us. Don't wait for tomorrow, don't try to relive yesterday. We are comfortable in our skin when we can just be ourselves, and we give comfort and stability to others. Today is what we have, and this stage in life is the best place to be. Live it well. RC

HopePrayer

I thank You for each new day, Lord, and for each new season. Would You please keep me focused on this season, on this day? Help me to embrace it and to live it well.

Letting Go

> *Don't worry about anything; instead,*
> *pray about everything. Tell God what you need,*
> *and thank him for all he has done.*

PHILIPPIANS 4:6 NLT

HopeMinute

I was having a bit of a tough time. I was putting my oldest daughter Annie on an airplane for a three-month internship near Atlanta. I've been told that this is a good thing for both of us. They say it is part of the "letting go" that all parents must go through.

Well, I don't care what they say—it still hurts.

I knew I would miss her terribly. As she gets older, my job as a parent is to trust God to care for her, even when I am not there or able to. I am to leave her in His faithful hands.

Even though my situation is certainly not as difficult or trying as many, I think the job of letting go in any situation is basically the same. I know that with all your heart you want to just do something to make things better and protect your child. Sometimes you can. Sometimes you cannot.

I encourage you to let go and place your trust and your hope in a plan bigger and more perfect than your own. God loves your child, and He loves you, more than you could ever imagine. Let go and relax in Him.   RC

HopePrayer

Lord, these are Your kids. These are Your situations. I entrust them all to You, *trusting* You to help me relax and watch You work. You do such a better job with them than I ever could.

Make the Most of This Day

> *Thanks be to God for his indescribable gift!*
>
> 2 Corinthians 9:15 NIV

HopeMinute

Babies are amazing. Place a newborn infant in any adult's arms and that adult will turn all their attention to that tiny new life. To hold a baby is to feel an incredible sense of joy. I miss that.

I was present for the birth of all my children. With each child I was again overwhelmed with the miracle of birth and the beauty of each little body. In each new child we see everything that is good, a projection of life and all its possibilities. I am sure my parents had the same sense of wonder when they held me.

We all have the same beginning. Regardless of age or situation, we all have the same amount of time in each day—twenty-four hours for you, twenty-four hours for me. Each day is full of possibilities.

What will you do with your next twenty-four hours? Marvel at the gift of having this day, take advantage of each moment, cherish each person that crosses your path, enjoy the blessings. Will you make the most of it?

RC

HopePrayer

Oh God, how thrilling that life begins so sweetly as in a tiny baby! And do You really see me as precious and tender as those babies? I am overwhelmed, God. Overwhelmed. Help me to make the most of this day You have given me.

I Can't Do This

HopeWord

> *I pray also that you will have a greater*
> *understanding in your heart so you will know*
> *the hope to which he has called us and that you*
> *will know how rich and glorious are the*
> *blessings God has promised his holy people.*

EPHESIANS 1:18 NCV

HopeMinute

Stressed, overwhelmed, concerned, helpless, uncertain, and depressed are all words I have overheard a lot recently. People are feeling the effects of an uncertain economy. Parents are worrying about how they are going to feed their families let alone pay those seemingly endless bills. Children are in need of antibiotics to treat infections. And the list goes on.

When our daughter Abby was being treated for a brain tumor in 2004, I experienced many of those emotions. There were times when I couldn't imagine how I would get through the day. One particular day, the stress felt like a great weight on my shoulders—like an actual extra weight.

What did I do? I called out to God for help. I simply collapsed on a chair and said, "I can't do this." And then I waited. His answer was a little unsettling, humbling, and yet completely clear to me. It was almost too good to be true! "You're right, you can't do it...but I can."

Was I able to go forth with a Pollyanna smile on my face the rest of the day? Probably not. The mountain of laundry was still there. Abby was still dealing with a spiking fever. The baby was still sick. We were countless days behind in schoolwork, housework, and everything else.

It's difficult to describe the overwhelming peace I felt when I realized that it wasn't about my ability to get through the difficult circumstances of my life. It was all about the God of the Universe who can handle anything and everything. My hope and prayer for you today is that you will meet God in a personal way and feel that same peace.

AO

HopePrayer

Lord, where did I ever get the idea I was supposed to be able to handle the weight of life all by myself? I *can't*. You can. You come to meet me personally, take up my burdens, and give me peace. Thank You for that. And please don't let me forget it.

An Invitation to Relax

HopeWord

> *Obsession with self in these matters is a dead end; attention*
> *to God leads us out into the open, into a spacious, free life.*
> ROMANS 8:6 THE MESSAGE

HopeMinute

One day, everything was fine. Then a headache, or a bloody nose, or a bump that wouldn't go away caused concern. This was followed by worry and then the tests...then more tests and consultations. Devastation. Fear. Uncertainty. Within a matter of days, life as you knew it came to a screeching halt.

If this, or something close to it, is the story of your family, I cannot even begin to imagine how sad you are feeling. In a short time, your world has been turned upside down. You've lost control. Future plans have been put on hold.

Severe sadness is the feeling we have when we experience loss. When a loved one is sick, dies, or simply

133

moves out of our lives, we lose something—particularly control over life. Resist the temptation to become obsessed with the situation. It leads to a dead end. It does not lead to relief or comfort, but to confusion and anxiety. Instead, relax and let go.

You do have some control left in your life. It has to do with what you pay attention to, what you allow your mind to focus on. Calm down as much as you can. Relax. Healing may take some time.

Allow God to work in and through others to help you. Allow God to work in your heart to teach you about Him, His grace, and His love. Allow God to bless you during this time of need in your life. He will send help. There is hope.   RC

HopePrayer

Lord, keep my mind focused on You. When I look around at my problems, they consume me. But when my eyes are on You, my problems recede. Take my face in Your hands like a small child so I will focus my eyes on You.

With Gratitude

*Let the word of Christ dwell in you richly as you
teach and admonish one another with all wisdom,
and as you sing psalms, hymns and spiritual songs
with gratitude in your hearts to God.*

COLOSSIANS 3:16 NIV

I shared an evening with a friend who was working
with God to heal her traumatic childhood. Her story
was tough, and she had a hard time trusting that anything good was meant for her; indeed, she had a hard
time trusting God, period. But after much interven-
tion, she was able to come to the point of hearing God
for herself, understanding why He had allowed what
He did, and what good had come to her because of it.
That is the long and rocky path many of us have walked
to find freedom.

I believe that when we come to the point of truly understanding how tragedy can result in significant growth, we are able to be grateful for it. Gratitude for the tough times indicates that we have come to grips with the situation and that healing is taking place.

My own childhood was traumatic as well, but somehow, I have always known that I wouldn't be me without it. I required much healing, but I know without that trauma I would not have the compassion, or tenderness, or other qualities God has cultivated in me specifically through the pain and the loss.

No doubt we can find it difficult to be grateful when things are really bad. No doubt the bad things do not always make sense. However, it's also true that those bad times often hold unforeseeable growth in our heart, in our character, in our relationship with God. If we can only surrender to the hard times and find the treasure in them, God will bless us and guide us in our search. He will infuse us with gratitude.

SC

HopePrayer

Lord, I think I'm understanding that the tougher the times, the more growth there is (if I let You do it). Thank You for these trials and for the good You bring from them. Please continue my growth, and increase my gratitude. I love You so much.

Through God's Eyes

> *Search me, O God, and know my heart;*
> *test me and know my anxious thoughts.*
> *See if there is any offensive way in me.*
>
> PSALM 139:23–24 NIV

HopeMinute

When you look in the mirror, what do you think? How do you see yourself? New clothes and styles may help mask the issues for a while. But if you want permanent change, you need to learn to see yourself through God's eyes. God "has covered me with clothes of salvation and wrapped me with a coat of goodness, like a bridegroom dressed for his wedding, like a bride dressed in jewels" (Isaiah 61:10 ncv). He sees us as beautiful.

How easy it is to believe what some people may say—that we aren't beautiful. How easy it is to remember the lack of affirmation we received as a child and the feeling that we don't measure up. How easy it is to consider these lies to be the truth about who we really are. We often fall victim to the world's marketing pitch that we must have that new product or look a certain way to be acceptable. That is categorically incorrect.

When I pray for people, I often pray that they see themselves through God's eyes. If we can do that, it can change everything. We will no longer see flaws and imperfections. We will see ourselves loved unconditionally for exactly who we are, as people with whom God desires a relationship. Imagine that—God wants to hang out with us! Wow.

The next time you look in the mirror, remember to try to see yourself as God does. Meditate and focus on that image. Allow His love to change the way you look at yourself.

RC

HopePrayer

Dear God, I ask You to show me how *You* see me. Give me eyes to see myself more clearly, and remind me of how beautiful I am in Your eyes.

Enjoyment

> *So I commend the enjoyment of life, because*
> *nothing is better for a man under the sun*
> *than to eat and drink and be glad. Then joy*
> *will accompany him in his work all the days*
> *of the life God has given him under the sun.*

ECCLESIASTES 8:15 NIV

HopeMinute

Don't you love being around people who love life? I do. They walk with a bounce, speak with enthusiasm, and smile a lot. Such people can scarcely contain their enthusiasm in whatever they do. They embrace both the joys and the challenges of life. They understand that it's not really about them anyway.

One of the most noticeable attributes of these life-loving people is how sincerely they enjoy other people. They know how to listen, but they also speak boldly.

They love relationships. They love their friends. Others seem improved just by being around them.

What's their secret? While many elements play a role, three stand out: optimism, balance, and perspective. These people show optimism in how they think of themselves and especially how they see others. They find the best in both. They show balance by loving what they do, but also by not being obsessed with it. And they have the right perspective. They enjoy life to the fullest, but they have a humility that comes from understanding that it is all a gift. They focus on others, not on themselves.

Try being a life-loving person this week. Relax. Focus on others. Look forward to Friday instead of dreading Monday. Enjoy life.   RC

HopePrayer

Lord, this life You've given me, You gave me to enjoy. With all its trials, You want joy to accompany me. Lord, please renew my enjoyment. Thank You, for this life, for despite all its struggles, my life is still a tremendous blessing.

What Hope Is

> *May the God of hope fill you with all joy and peace as*
> *you trust in him, so that you may overflow with hope.*

ROMANS 15:13 NIV

Hope is...knowing that a positive outcome awaits and being okay that it might look different than you thought.

Hope is...not only expecting a dream to come true, but having a deep assurance that it's within your reach.

Hope is...saying you can improve and that you always get better with practice.

Hope is...knowing that you can.

Hope is...knowing that someone loves you.

Hope is...realizing that you don't need to know all the answers, God already does.

Hope is...looking to the future with joy and having expectations of better things to come.

Hope is...knowing that miracles still happen everyday.

Hope is...something that never abandons you. Even when your life is filled with sadness and disappointment, a spark remains inside to help you get through the rough times.

Hope is...a very powerful medicine.

Hope is...often beyond our understanding but always real and true.

Hope is...one of God's greatest gifts to you, because it's the magic that inspires you to keep living.   RC

HopePrayer

Thank You, Lord, for showing me the power of hope. Remind me when any trouble comes my way, that hope is available—in You. Thank You for being my hope.

About the Authors

Rob and Susan Cottrell have been married for almost twenty-five years and have five grown and growing kids. Rob is the founder and president of HopeKids (hopekids.org), an organization providing hope for children with life-threatening medical conditions and their families. Susan is a writer, speaker, retreat leader, and author of *The Heart-Connected Life* (heartconnectedlife.org).